LET'S-READ-AND-FIND-OUT SCIENCE®

STAGE 1

Where Do CHICKS Come From?

By Amy E. Sklansky • Illustrated by Pam Paparone

HarperCollinsPublishers

For Nicole, Cindy, and Steve, with thanks
—A.E.S.

For Richard
—P.P.

The *Let's-Read-and-Find-Out Science* book series was originated by Dr. Franklyn M. Branley, Astronomer Emeritus and former Chairman of the American Museum–Hayden Planetarium, and was formerly co-edited by him and Dr. Roma Gans, Professor Emeritus of Childhood Education, Teachers College, Columbia University. Text and illustrations for each of the books in the series are checked for accuracy by an expert in the relevant field. For more information about Let's-Read-and-Find-Out Science books, write to HarperCollins Children's Books, 1350 Avenue of the Americas, New York, NY 10019, or visit our website at www.letsreadandfindout.com.

Library of Congress Cataloging-in-Publication Data
Sklansky, Amy E.
  Where do chicks come from? / by Amy E. Sklansky ; illustrated by Pam Paparone.
    p.   cm. — (Let's-read-and-find-out science. Stage 1.)
  Summary: Describes what happens day-by-day for the three weeks from the time a hen lays an egg until the baby chick hatches.
  ISBN 0-06-028892-2 — ISBN 0-06-028893-0 (lib. bdg.)
  ISBN 0-06-445212-3 (pbk.)
1. Chickens—Life cycles—Juvenile literature. [1. Chickens. 2. Eggs.] I. Paparone, Pamela, ill. II. Title. III. Series.
SF487.5.S54 2005   2003007711
636.5—dc21

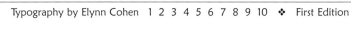

Typography by Elynn Cohen   1 2 3 4 5 6 7 8 9 10   ❖   First Edition

Where Do
CHICKS
Come From?

This is an egg. You've seen eggs before, but this one is different. In three weeks, a chick will hatch out of this egg.

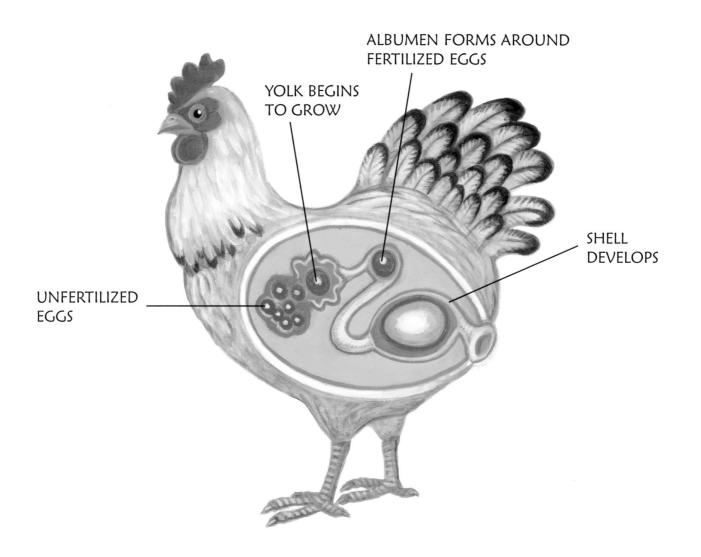

ALBUMEN FORMS AROUND
FERTILIZED EGGS

YOLK BEGINS
TO GROW

SHELL
DEVELOPS

UNFERTILIZED
EGGS

An egg begins as a tiny white spot inside the mother chicken, the hen. There may be many tiny eggs inside the hen at one time. A yellow yolk grows around each egg.

Then the father chicken, the rooster, mates with the hen.
His sperm joins the growing egg. This is called fertilization.
Soon, a clear jelly-like egg white, or albumen, grows around
the yolk. Finally, a hard shell forms. The egg is ready to be laid.

The hen lays the egg. Over the next few days, she lays several more eggs. The hen sits on top of the eggs to keep them warm. As soon as the eggs are warm, the chicks start growing.

9

Inside the warm egg is everything a chick needs to grow.

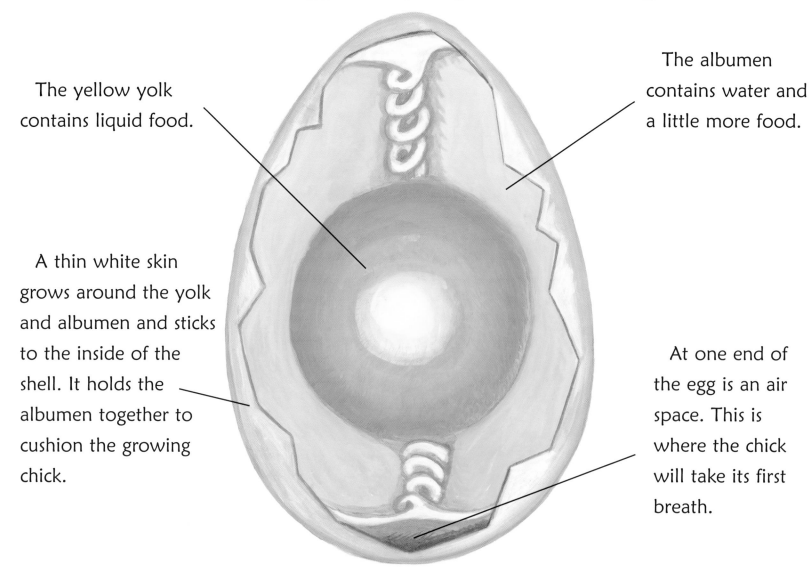

The yellow yolk contains liquid food.

The albumen contains water and a little more food.

A thin white skin grows around the yolk and albumen and sticks to the inside of the shell. It holds the albumen together to cushion the growing chick.

At one end of the egg is an air space. This is where the chick will take its first breath.

The egg you eat for breakfast could never grow into a chick because it was never fertilized. Otherwise, all parts inside the egg are the same.

The hen has warmed her eggs for three days now. Inside, the chicks are growing.

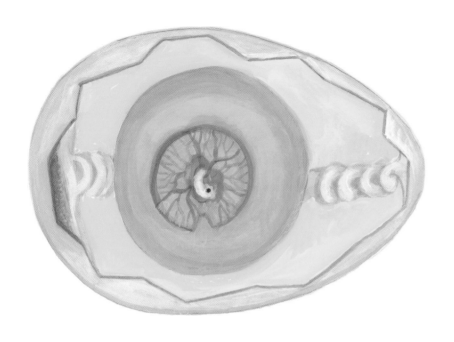

DAY 3: The chick looks like the letter C with a dark spot in the middle. This spot is its heart. The heart pumps blood. The blood carries water and food from the yolk and albumen to the growing chick. The chick's waste collects in a small sac.

DAY 5: The chick's head is now half as big as its body, and its eyes are very large. Its tail has begun to grow. Wings and legs are forming.

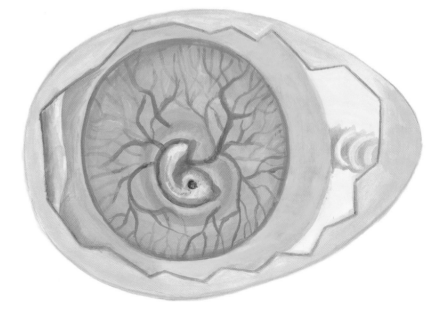

Briefly, the hen leaves the eggs to find food and water. She quickly returns to warm them again.

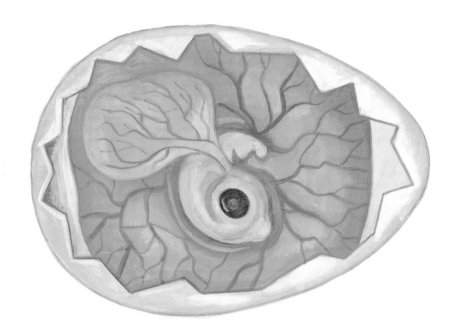

DAY 7: The chick is only one inch long—about as long as your big toe. Even so, it is already starting to look like a chicken. The chick's eyes, stomach, brain, and toes have started to grow. A beak has started to grow, too, but it is very soft. The chick's wings are folded across its chest.

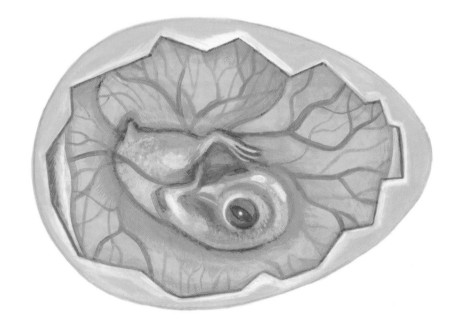

DAY 10: Every day, the chick uses up more of the food from the yolk. The chick lies on its back inside the egg. Its wings, legs, and beak are fully grown.

Sometimes the hen turns the eggs over. She keeps them warm on all sides.

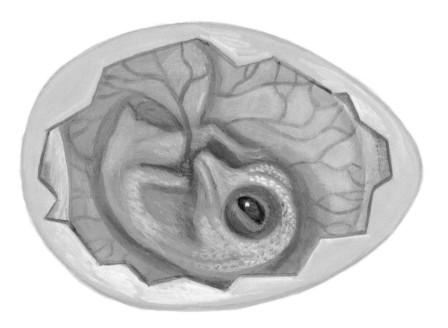

DAY 11: The chick can open and close its beak now. It wiggles and bends within the albumen. Tiny bumps appear all over the chick's skin. In a few days feathers will grow from these bumps.

DAY 14: The chick is tightly curled inside the egg. It turns to lie on its side. As the chick uses up more and more of the yolk and albumen, the waste bag expands. The chick has grown a special bump on the end of its beak. This is called the egg tooth.

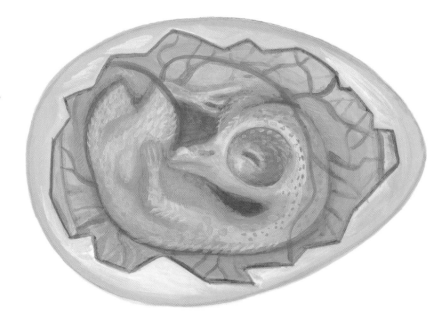

The hen clucks softly and turns her eggs again. The chicks
are learning to recognize the sound of their mother's voice.
The hen no longer leaves her eggs. She will not eat or
drink again until after they have hatched.

DAY 18: The chick has grown so big that it touches the inside of the shell on every side. Soft feathers called down cover its head and body. The chick uses up the last of the yolk. The yolk will give the chick energy to hatch and then rest for a few days without eating.

DAY 20: The chick practices breathing. In one day it will hatch.

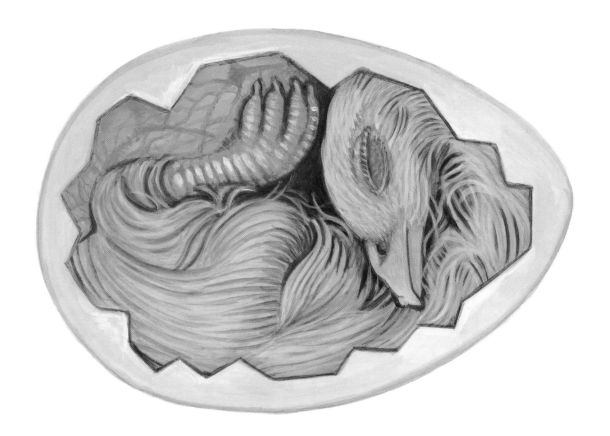

Inside the eggshell, the chick pecks a hole into the air space at the end of the egg. It takes its first breath and goes, "Cheep! Cheep!"

"Cluck, cluck," answers the hen.

The next day, the chick pecks a tiny hole in the shell using its egg tooth. This is tough work for the chick. After making the hole, the chick sleeps for a few hours.

23

When the chick wakes up, it pecks for hours. It pecks a circle around the inside of the shell.

Next, it pushes hard against one side of the shell with its feet. Then it pushes hard against the other side with its neck and shoulders.

Crack! The chick has hatched! The shell and the dried-up waste sac fall away. The chick doesn't need its egg tooth anymore. In a few days, it will fall off.

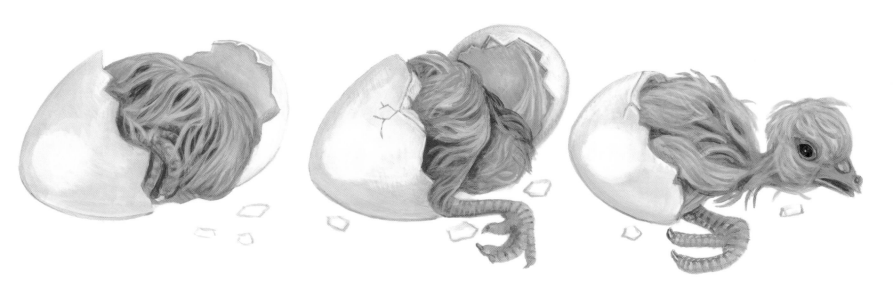

The chick is tired. It rests its wobbly legs as the other chicks finish hatching.

The hen fluffs her feathers and spreads her wings to cover and warm her new chicks. The babies nestle close to their mother and sleep. As they rest, their down dries. Their legs and necks grow stronger.

Hours later, the fluffy chick is the first to run out from beneath its mother's wings. The others soon follow. Together, the hen and her new chicks search for food in the barnyard.

FIND OUT MORE ABOUT EGGS AND CHICKS

• Can You Break an Egg?

Try this with an uncooked egg and a large bowl. Hold the egg in the palm of your hand over the bowl. Now squeeze the egg as hard as you can. The egg should not break. (The bowl is there just in case there is a tiny crack in the egg—the only reason it should break in your hand.) Like the pressure from the palm of your hand, a hen's weight spreads out evenly over the rounded shape of the eggshell when she sits on an egg. This ensures that her egg won't break.

• Inside an Egg

Ask an adult to help you break an uncooked egg into a small bowl. Look closely. Can you identify the yellow yolk and the gooey, clear albumen? Now do you see what look like twisted white strings? These are called the *chalazae* (pronounced kuh-*lay*-zee). They help keep the yolk in place and protected within the egg.

Look inside the shell. Can you see the air sac attached to the wider end of the egg? After you have finished your observations, you might want to make scrambled eggs or an omelet.

• Roll an Egg

For this activity you will need some newspaper and an uncooked egg. Spread out a piece of newspaper on the floor or tabletop. Place the egg on the paper and give it a gentle push. Watch to see how it rolls. Does it roll fast and straight like a soccer ball, or does it wobble and move in a circular motion? Why do you think this is? Do you think the egg's shape makes it easier or harder for the hen to take care of it?

• Enjoy These Stories Starring Chicks:

LITTLE CHICK'S FRIEND DUCKLING by Mary DeBall Kwitz, illustrated by Bruce Degen

DAISY COMES HOME by Jan Brett

TIPPY-TOE CHICK, GO! by George Shannon, illustrated by Laura Dronzek

THE CHICK AND THE DUCKLING by Mirra Ginsburg, illustrated by Jose Aruego and Ariane Dewey

GOOD MORNING, CHICK by Mirra Ginsburg, illustrated by Byron Barton

THE CHICK THAT WOULDN'T HATCH by Claire Daniel, illustrated by Lisa Campbell Ernst